FOREWORD

How can I know if I'm doing the right things as a parent? What is the definition of success in parenting?

We all want to know the answers to these questions, don't we? This book offers a bold, clear answer:

"Success is not helping our kids be what they want to be. Success is helping our kids be what God wants them to be."

These words summarize a passion and calling that Awana® and Dr. Rob Rienow share together – that parents understand and acquire God's grand vision for our homes as the primary spiritual training ground for our children!

You are holding this book because, at some level, you are developing a vision for your child's life that goes beyond the cultural norm. You are seeing that the ultimate measure of your success in parenting is not your child's future income, education or social status. Instead, it is whether your child gets safely home to heaven and is equipped to lead future generations of your family there too.

For Awana, this vision for your child's life is embodied in an ideal we call **Modern-Day Joseph™**. Inspired by Joseph of the Old Testament in the Bible, this is a young person who comes to know, love and serve God as a youth and lives out a vibrant, visible faith in a morally hostile, destructive environment.

The ministry of Awana is here to help you raise a modern-day Joseph! We do this by encouraging and equipping you to be the primary spiritual leader of your children, and also by supplying churches with proven children's ministry programs that complement your discipleship efforts at home.

Please visit www.awana.org to learn more about raising a modern-day Joseph and how Awana can help you accomplish God's grand vision for your home.

INTRODUCTION

Let's begin with a question.

When your son or daughter leaves your home someday, which one of the following would you want most for them?

> a) To be successful academically.
> b) To be successful athletically.
> c) To be successful socially.
> d) To be a person of faith and character.

Personally, I would like to have another option, e) All of the above. But if you could only have one, which one would you choose? You most likely said that faith and character are most important. At least it seems like the "right answer."

Let me change the question a bit. Which of the following parenting issues gets the best of your time, effort, money, anxiety and planning?

> a) Academics.
> b) Athletics.
> c) Social life.
> d) Faith and character development.

INTRODUCTION

TABLE OF CONTENTS

Introduction 6

Searching for Purpose: Chapter 1 12

Journey to the Heart: Chapter 2 18

God's Purpose for Your Family: Chapter 3 30

Four God-Filled Moments: Chapter 4 40

Rediscovering Family Worship: Chapter 5 52

Practicing Family Worship: Chapter 6 62

Don't Go Alone: Chapter 7 82

Conclusion 88

If you had to rank them in order of the amount of time, money and effort that goes into each one, what would come out on top? What would come out on the bottom? I asked myself these questions in my role as a father, and the answers were challenging. The thing that I claimed was most important to me – the faith and character development of my children – was often at the bottom of my actual priority list.

Let's imagine that all of my children turn out to be smart, athletic, popular, polite and hardworking. It would seem that they would be poised for all the success the world has to offer. But what if they didn't love God and know His plan for their lives? Most important of all, what if they don't get safely home to heaven?

There is nothing wrong with being great at sports, getting good grades or being well-liked. The danger is that if these things become our focus, we can completely miss the things that truly matter.

God has a grand vision for your home. He put each and every person in your family together for a purpose, and He gave you children for a reason. God didn't do all this just to have you "survive" being in the same house together for 18 years. I pray that as you read this book, God's grand vision for your home will come into focus for you.

There are two basic types of parents who will actually read a book on parenting. The first is the mom or dad who reads everything on parenting. They are the resident parenting experts in their neighborhoods, and they seem to be on top of their game at all times.

The rest of us are in the other category. A lot of days we are at our wits' end. We have reached the point where we are so desperate that we are actually willing to read a book! Don't be discouraged. As you read, I hope that you will be able to relate to my ups and downs as a father. Take heart! Because of the grace of God, it is never too late to change, grow and become the parent God wants you to be.

I believe God wants to expand your vision for your family. I believe He wants to inspire and refresh your heart for the things that matter most. This journey is going to take us to the Bible. The Bible is a divinely inspired book, and in its pages God reveals to us His grand vision and purpose for our lives.

Everyone's family is different, but God's purpose for every family is the same. No matter what kind of family you came from, or what kind of family you are in right now,

God has chosen to put you together for a reason. Would you like to know what it is?

Open your hearts, prepare for God to do something new and join me in discovering God's grand vision for your home.

SEARCHING FOR PURPOSE

Imagine that you are at a mall. A television crew is doing random interviews with people. The reporter makes his way toward you, and before you know it, you are looking into a camera. The reporter asks you the following question, "In your opinion, what is the purpose of family?"

Awkward pause. You mentally scramble for something meaningful, or at least witty, to say. Before you know it, you blurt out, "Love." Not bad. Thankfully, the reporter moves on to the next person. Later that evening you see yourself on the local news. Other people at the mall that day offered some good answers as well. "Support." "Comfort." "Raising kids to be productive members of society."

I believe that every parent should be able to answer this question without hesitation. If we are not clear about the purpose of our families, how can we expect to be successful?

If we want to know the purpose of family, we have to go to the Creator of family. God is the one who made us.

He is the one who designed us male and female, and gave us the institution of marriage. He is the one who made it possible for us to have children. We are made in His image, and He invites us into the miracle of creation. And what a miracle it is, when God uses a man and a woman together to create a new physical, spiritual and immortal person. God is the one who gave us the assignment of being a parent. So what is the point? What purpose did He have in creating the family? The answer will unfold in the chapters ahead.

Our journey begins with a conversation that Jesus had with one of the religious leaders of His day. In Matthew 22:35-38, this religious leader pins Jesus down with one of the toughest questions of all time.

> *One of them, an expert in the law, tested Him with this question: "Teacher, which is the greatest commandment in the Law?" Jesus replied: "'Love the Lord your God with all your heart and with all your soul and with all your mind.' This is the first and greatest commandment."*

So the question is posed to Jesus, "If God calls us to do just one thing, what is it?"

Isn't it awesome that there is an actual answer to that question? There is a purpose to life! Jesus says that the reason you and I were created was so that we might love God with our whole being.

What would real life look like if we loved God with everything? We would talk with God in prayer throughout the day, speaking to Him and listening to what He says to us through His Word. We would sense a deep peace in our hearts, even when our lives seem to be falling apart. We would be drawn to reading our Bibles, more powerfully than we are drawn to hobbies or the TV. We would seek to be obedient to God in every area of our lives and hate our sin. Our hearts would be filled with compassion for those in need, and we would feel a sense of urgency to share the gospel with those who don't know Christ. Do these things describe your life? These things are not always true of me … but I wish they were.

The philosopher Blaise Pascal illustrated our need for God by suggesting that every person is created with a God-shaped hole or "vacuum" in our hearts. We are born with a void inside. We are created for a personal love relationship with our Father God. If we don't have it, our hearts are restless, our lives are unfulfilled, and we keep trying to find something to give us meaning. We try to fill the void with anything and everything we can.

The world tells us, "If you owned that car or that house, then you would be happy." "If you had that position in the company or had that office, then you could feel good about yourself." "If you could have a relationship with someone as gorgeous as the person on the magazine cover, then life would be thrilling." The world tells us that if we take enough of all that stuff and shove it into the hole inside our hearts, we will be satisfied.

As you look back on your life, how have you tried to fill that God-shaped hole? Did it work? Was your feeling of fulfillment lasting or fleeting?

We were created for a love relationship with God. That is what life is all about. Jesus Christ died on the cross for our sins and rose from the dead so that we can be restored to that love relationship with our Creator.

Nothing else and no one else can satisfy the craving that our hearts have for peace, joy and significance. Many people spend their lives failing to find contentment, all because they are not in a love relationship with God through faith in Jesus Christ. God wants to use your family to point your children to Jesus from the very beginning.

JOURNEY TO THE HEART | 2

JOURNEY TO THE HEART

Do you want your son or daughter to be successful in life? As we discovered in the last chapter, Jesus said that the most important thing in all of life, for you and for your children, is to love God! That is success. Success is not helping our kids be what they want to be. Success is helping our kids be what **God** wants them to be.

In order for us to fully understand what Jesus was saying, we need to refer to the Old Testament passage where that command is found. In Deuteronomy 6:4-5 it says:

> *Hear, O Israel: The LORD our God, the LORD is one. Love the LORD your God with all your heart and with all your soul and with all your strength.*

Too often we stop there. But the subsequent verses show us how to make this Great Commandment a reality.

In verse 6, God focuses our attention, once again, on the centrality of our hearts.

These commandments that I give you today are to be upon your hearts.

God was very clear from the beginning that following Him was never supposed to be simply a list of dos and don'ts. God does not like you more or less depending on how well you follow a list. He is looking for something deeper – your heart and the hearts of your children. Why? Because He knows that you will naturally follow after what you love. If you love watching TV, no one will have to remind you to do it. You will just naturally gravitate toward the remote. If you love shopping, you won't need anyone to keep you accountable to go to the mall.

I have to admit that when I am struggling in my walk with God, it is because of a love problem. When I am not taking time to pray and read my Bible, the basic problem isn't discipline – it's a lack of love. Discipline may be a part of it, but we naturally pursue the things that we love. This is why faith is first and foremost a matter of the heart … because when God has our hearts, He has everything else.

But what best prepares our hearts for a relationship with God? How and where do our hearts get shaped? The answer is our homes and families – more powerfully and more permanently than anything else on earth.

Think about a family experience you had as a child that impacted your heart in a positive way. How did that experience build character in your life?

Or perhaps you experienced things in your home that were hurtful or damaging. All of us, even if we come from healthy families, have areas of lingering "heart damage" from things we experienced when we were young.

In the same ways, the hearts of your children are – right now – being formed by your family life. Your daily schedule is teaching their hearts what is truly important about life. Their hearts are being molded by the discussions that take place (or fail to take place) around the dinner table. Their worldview, morality and faith are all taking shape right before your eyes … whether you see it or not.

God has granted to us, as parents, overwhelming power and influence in the hearts of our kids. A teacher at school cannot train and reach my kid's heart. At best they can scratch the surface. A Bible teacher at a Christian school cannot train and reach my kid's heart. At best they can give good knowledge, encouragement and personal care. A youth pastor at a great church does not possess anywhere near the power that I will have over the heart of my teenager.

If you have teenagers, it may appear that your influence has decreased. It may appear that your teenager looks to friends, music or even other adults for direction. Don't be fooled. You still hold more sway, for good or for ill, than anyone else in your teenager's life. I can personally testify to this truth after 11 years in full-time youth ministry.

Have you ever noticed that we live in an age of delegation parenting? If we want our kids to learn math, we get a tutor. If we want them to learn a sport, we get a coach. If we want them to learn Jesus, we get a Sunday school teacher.

Don't misunderstand. I am not against teachers, tutors, coaches, Sunday school teachers, or children's and youth ministry workers. Many other caring adults can assist us in our parenting journey. But we must realize that God has given to moms and dads the primary responsibility and power to shape the hearts of children. We must not delegate it to others!

Imagine a teenage girl is walking through the halls at school, and a boy comes up to her and says, "Wow, are you ugly. No one is ever going to marry you." What a horrible, hurtful thing to hear!

Now imagine that girl goes home, and her father looks up from his newspaper and says, "Wow, are you ugly. No one is ever going to marry you."

Is there any difference between these two insults? You bet there is! Those words, coming from the mouth of a father, impact the deepest places of her heart.

The power of a parent to wound a child's heart is extreme. Those who are closest to us have the greatest power to hurt us, and as we will see in a moment, the greatest power to build us up.

Do you remember the feelings you experienced the first time you held your newborn child? I recall thinking about how God had entrusted me with this tiny, fragile person. I know it is a bit morbid, but I also had the fearful thought that I could drop my child, causing serious damage. My child's life was literally in my hands at that moment.

Every parent is aware of how physically fragile our children are in those early years. (Now that my oldest son is getting bigger I am starting to worry about him hurting me when we wrestle!) What we may fail to realize is that the hearts of our children are just as fragile today as their bodies were when they were born. Our careless words, harsh treatment and angry outbursts can leave wounds that last a lifetime.

On the other hand, no one can compete with the power that a father and mother have to nurture their children, to build their character and to lead them to Jesus. Children need a home in which they are confident that Mom and Dad love God, love each other and love them. These "three loves" provide the strongest foundation for a family and for a child's life.

When the three loves are in place, children grow into teenagers and young adults who say, "I don't need to mess around sexually in order to find acceptance. I am accepted." "I am a valuable person, no matter what kind of car I drive, clothes I wear or grades I get." "I don't need to use drugs to mask the pain I have in my life, because if I need to run away from pain, I can go home. Home is safe."

But too often the family is the cause of the pain. Hundreds of teenagers that I served over the years in youth ministry were spinning out of control because they had terrible relationships with their parents.

Millions of children are suffering from the pain of divorce. I shared in that pain as my parents divorced when

I was in high school. Even though God gave my mother grace and strength to be a single parent, my heart still desired to be in a home where mom and dad loved each other.

No matter what marriage situation you are in right now, God wants to help you be the parent He created you to be. Offer your heart and life to the Lord in prayer. Ask Him for His strength and wisdom. And don't be afraid to reach out to others for help. Get connected with a Bible-believing church. A Christian community can be the greatest support in your parenting journey.

I try to communicate the three love statements to my kids. One night, as I was putting my then 5-year-old daughter to bed, I told her, "Lissy, I want you to know that Dad loves Jesus, Dad loves Mom and Dad loves you." She asked a great question: "Dad, why am I last?" At first I laughed, but I realized she was asking an honest question.

I responded, "Lissy, I am so glad you asked. Do you think that if I didn't love your mom, that I could be the best dad for you?" She shook her head. I continued, "And do you think that if I didn't love Jesus, that I could be the best husband for Mom?" Again, she shook her head. "So,

In the first chapter, we learned from Jesus that the purpose of life is to love God with all our heart, soul and strength. In this chapter, we discovered that this love God desires for us is first and foremost a matter of the heart … and that is where the family comes in. Our hearts are shaped most powerfully at home, and as we continue to walk through Deuteronomy 6 in the next chapter, God's purpose for our families will become clear.

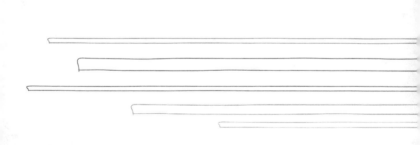

GOD'S PURPOSE FOR YOUR FAMILY

Have you ever wondered WHY God gave you your children? You are about to find out.

According to Jesus, the most important commandment in the Scriptures is to love God with all our heart, soul and strength. But what are we supposed to do with that? The commandment sounds good. It even feels inspiring! But where do we begin putting this Great Commandment into practice?

God knew that we would ask this question, and so He answered it in Deuteronomy 6:5-7a:

> *Love the LORD your God with all your heart and with all your soul and with all your strength. These commandments that I give you today are to be upon your hearts. Impress them on your children.*

So what is the first action step for following the Great Commandment, according to God's Word? You begin by impressing the hearts of your children with a love for God.

I believe that these five words, *impress them on your children*, teach that God's primary plan of evangelism and discipleship is from parent to child.

Why did God give you your children? He entrusted them to you so that you might lead them to know, love and serve Him. God gave you your children so that you would help them get safely home to heaven. He has given you the mission of training your children so that they can be saved and have the opportunity to bring many others to heaven with them.

The purpose of parenting (and grandparenting!) is to impress the hearts of our children with a love for God. Loving God is the purpose of life, and we are to lead our children to it.

Imagine if your children inherited a terminal disease from you. Wouldn't you do everything in your power to find a cure so that they might live? This is not an imaginary situation. Our kids have inherited from us something much worse than a terminal illness. They have inherited a sinful nature that guarantees them an eternity separated from God. Our most important parenting mission, then, is to lead our children to salvation by God's grace, through faith in Jesus Christ.

The statistics are overwhelmingly clear. If we don't lead our children intentionally, passionately and fervently, to know God and love Him while they are in our homes, the likelihood of them giving their lives to Christ later in life is slim. In fact, only 10 percent of all the Christians in the United States become believers after the age of 18.[1] Why is this? I would suggest that it is because God has given the greatest responsibility and power for evangelism to parents.

I believe that if a young person grows up in a godly nation, a godly school, a godly church, but an ungodly home, then the chances are slim that young person will get safely home to heaven and make a difference in the world for Christ. On the other hand, if a young person grows up in an ungodly nation, in an ungodly school, in an ungodly church (God forbid), but a godly home, then the chances are good that child will get home to heaven and make a difference in the world for Christ.

We are now prepared to answer our big question. What is the purpose of family? **God created your family to be a discipleship center**. God made your family so that you would help each other to love Him more. You are together so that you might help each other discover Christ, grow in

---

[1] George Barna, *Transforming Children Into Spiritual Champions.*

Him together and together make a difference in the world for Him.

A discipleship center … is this the central passion and purpose of your family? What kind of "center" has your family been? Many families today are sports centers, activity centers, wealth-building centers or scholastic centers. If you had to fill in the blank, what would you say has been the central purpose and focus of your family?

Perhaps you are a part of a church that has "discipleship small groups" or "growth groups." These are groups of people who gather together regularly to encourage each other spiritually, study the Bible and pray for one another. Being part of a group like this can make a big difference in a person's spiritual journey. Did you know that God wants every person to be in a discipleship small group from birth? He calls them families!

God's grand vision for your family is that you would help one another love and follow Him more fully every day. In Matthew 28:19, Jesus told His followers to *make disciples.* This passage is known as the Great Commission. As a Christian parent, my Great Commission to make disciples begins with my children, the immortal souls that God has entrusted to me.

As I consider these truths, a question haunts me. What am I doing daily with this power and responsibility to impress the hearts of my kids with a love for God? As a pastor, am I putting more time and energy into leading the ministries at church than I am in leading my home? When was the last time I took one of my kids out for ice cream to read the Bible together?

I plan and lead programs at church in an attempt to help people grow spiritually. When was the last time I planned a time with my own family to help my wife and kids grow spiritually? What a tragedy it would be if my legacy as a Christian man was time spent in spiritual leadership at church while failing to be a spiritual leader at home!

My life changed in the summer of 2004. God brought me face-to-face with some painful realities in my life. Up until that point, I would have told you that I was a man of priorities. If you had asked me, "Rob, what are your priorities as a Christian man?" I would have given you all the right answers. My first priority was my relationship with God. My second was my relationship with my wife, and then third was my relationship with my children. My fourth life priority was making a difference in the lives of those around me, including my ministry at church, my neighborhood, etc. I had everything in the right order. God, wife, kids and others. Sounds great!

I told myself that not only were these things my stated priorities, but that they were my real life priorities. If my boss called me on the phone with a crisis, and my wife called me on the phone with a crisis, where would I go? Church or home? Easy. I would go home. Why? Because I was a man of priorities! But during that life-changing summer, the Lord posed a different series of questions to my heart. "Rob, what are your priorities when there is no crisis? What gets the best of your heart, passion, energy and leadership each day?"

Asked that way, my four perfect priorities flipped upside down. The best of my heart, passion and energy went to work, then to my kids, then to my wife. And, in many ways, my personal walk with God came in last. I had to confess to the Lord that this was the true picture of my life. I had to confess this to my wife and to my kids. That summer God began a work in my heart and life, turning the best of my heart and ministry to my family. It wasn't too late for me, and it isn't too late for you.

If someone were to follow you around for a month and record how you spent your time, your money, your

daydreams, your creative thinking and your energies …
what would they conclude are your most important
priorities? What gets the best of you … not in crisis, but
daily? Does your family get your best, or the leftovers?

Changing your family will start with changing your
heart. Your children are learning every day what is most
important in life by watching you and listening to you. My
prayer is that God has inspired your heart as you have read
this chapter. I pray He has expanded your vision for your
family and called you to do everything in your power to
impress the hearts of your kids with a love for God.

But how can sinful people like us ever succeed at this?
How can we, with our problems, tempers and failures,
possibly lead the hearts of our kids to love God? God
knew we would ask this question. As we will discover in
the following chapter, the next verse we encounter in
Deuteronomy 6 gives us the perfect place to start.

FOUR GOD-FILLED MOMENTS

What's the secret? If God created our families to be discipleship centers, and He gave us our children to impress their hearts with a love for God, where do we start? In Deuteronomy 6:7, God lovingly gives us a practical "how-to" list for leading our kids in faith.

> ... *Talk about them* [the commands of God] *when you sit at home and when you walk along the road, when you lie down and when you get up.*

So what is the magical, mysterious formula for imperfect moms and dads to help their kids fall in love with God? What is the super-secret strategy? Talk with them! What a radical, revolutionary concept! God instructs parents to talk with their children about spiritual things. He then gives us four strategic times each day to carry out His instructions.

Is it important to be a good spiritual model for your children? Absolutely, and we will talk about that in later chapters. Is it essential to bring them to church? Of course, it is a key commitment of the Christian family. But God's Word speaks clearly to us as parents, that our mission to impress the hearts of our kids with a love for God must be rooted in *daily conversations and instruction* about spiritual things.

God gives us four times during each day as prime opportunities to reach the hearts of our kids. The first critical time is *when you sit at home.* You know, those times each night when everyone from the family is relaxing together, gathered around the dinner table or just sitting in an unhurried manner, chatting in the living room.

What? You don't have times like that? You are not alone. Life is faster than ever. Few families are ever simply "sitting at home" anymore.

Two years ago, I read this verse and was struck with a terrible feeling. My family of six was on the fast track of life. We rarely had times when we were sitting together at home. The exception was meals, and those few times were not filled with spiritual discussion. As I wrestled with this verse, I basically told God in prayer that because of my schedule I didn't have time to follow this instruction!

God was far more gracious with me than I deserved. God responded to that ridiculous prayer with a firm but gentle message: "Rob, if your schedule is preventing you from sitting at home and talking about Me with your family, then the schedule you have chosen is causing you to sin."

Ouch! I was not following the very first action point and responsibility that I had as a parent. I had to confess to God that He was right. Then Amy and I began to make changes in our family's schedule so that we could have time to sit at home with the family and talk about the things of God.

You may be saying, "OK, I can get my family to sit down together. But what do I do then? What will I say? How will it work?" For many centuries, this priority of spiritual time in the home has been called "family worship." In the next chapter we will dig deeper into the importance of this family worship time and talk about practical ways to make it engaging and meaningful for everyone in the family.

So, the first key moment of spiritual conversation is *when you sit at home*. The passage then goes on to give us the second key time of the day to talk about spiritual things with our kids, *when you walk along the road*. In ancient times, when you needed to get somewhere, you walked. Today, we drive. This refers to our transition times, our "in-between" times. God's Word says that these are prime moments to talk to our children about spiritual things, about who God is and about what it means to follow Him.

In my family, we are trying to develop the habit of having a brief, spiritually focused conversation each time we get in the car. Perhaps it is a prayer for the safety of our trip. Perhaps it is a quick review of a Bible passage we talked about in the morning. My goal is to take advantage of these opportunities given by God.

One morning, the family was driving me to work. We were one minute away from church and I realized that I had forgotten to have our "car talk." So I quickly said, "Kids, here is one of Daddy's favorite verses from the Bible: Philippians 2:5, *Your attitude should be the same as that of Christ Jesus*. What kind of attitude did Jesus have?"

They replied simply, "A good one."

I said, "Yes, a good one. (I guess I was expecting something more profound!) He was joyful. He was patient. So as we go through our day, let's remember that our attitudes should be the same as that of Christ Jesus. I love you. Have a good day." It was just a short spiritual touch, tagged on the last minute of our car ride.

At the end of the day, my wife picked me up and we drove to a friend's house for dinner. Amy and I got into an "honest and open marital interaction" (otherwise known as an argument) in the front seat of the car. Our voices were raised, and things were going in the wrong direction. From the back of the car, our 7-year-old called out, "Remember our verse!" That was not what I wanted to hear in that moment. I wanted to win the argument! But short spiritual touches make a difference. In this case, the verse came back to convict me as my child confronted my bad behavior.

The third and fourth key opportunities to talk with our kids about faith are *when you lie down and when you get up*. In other words, the first few moments and the last few moments of the day are powerful windows into the hearts of our kids. As a result, I am watching my schedule so that I can have a spiritual "touch point" with my kids every morning and every night. It is hard, and I am far from perfect. This is an area where I know what I ought to do, but struggle to do it. I get distracted so easily. I can miss these precious windows as I check my e-mail, pick up a book, clean the kitchen or work on a house project.

One powerful way to impact the hearts of your kids when they wake up or go to bed is through the ancient practice of blessing them. A blessing is a prayer of encouragement for your son or daughter. It is a statement spoken both to them and to God at the same time. For instance, saying, "God bless you today" is a simple example of an encouraging spiritual word spoken to your child, but also offered to God in prayer. We learn this powerful parenting tool from our heavenly Father, who regularly communicates "blessing" to His children. Immediately after God created Adam and Eve, He blessed them.

> *God blessed them and said to them, "Be fruitful and increase in number; fill the earth and subdue it." (Genesis 1:28a)*

This is the first of numerous blessings of God directly expressed to His children in the Scriptures. Dictionaries define a *blessing* as "the bestowal of good." In other words, we bless our children when we say, "I wish this for you. I give this vision to you. I desire this good thing for you." I believe that we need to resurrect this ancient and biblical concept of blessing our children.

The parents in the Bible clearly understood the power of blessing, and they practiced it. In the book of Genesis, we find a beautiful picture of a grandfather blessing his son and grandsons. You may know the story of how Joseph was taken from his father, Jacob, and sold into slavery in Egypt. After many years, they were reunited. Jacob then said to Joseph, who now had children of his own, "Bring me your children, please, so that I may bless them."

> Then he blessed Joseph and said, "May the God before whom my fathers Abraham and Isaac walked, the God who has been my shepherd all my life to this day, the Angel who has delivered me from all harm – may He bless these boys. May they be called by my name and the names of my fathers Abraham and Isaac, and may they increase greatly upon the earth." (Genesis 48:15-16)

Can you imagine how it would feel to have your grandfather put his hand on your head and speak words like this to you? God has given the power of blessing to parents and grandparents. The Bible talks about these blessings as having real emotional and spiritual power. They are not a magic formula or incantation, but rather this practice of blessing is a powerful spiritual tool that God has created for parents to reach the hearts of their kids.

I experienced this power firsthand as I was growing up. My mother blessed me at the start of every day. She would gently put her hand on me before I started my day, and she spoke words of blessing adapted from Numbers 6:24-26. I can still hear her voice saying:

"May the Lord bless you and keep you. May the Lord make His face to shine upon you, and give you peace, all the days of your life, my son."

Now, it is my honor to take the legacy of blessing that my mother shared with me and share it with my children. Each night, before putting my children to bed, I place my hand on them and speak those same words. It has become a powerful spiritual moment between me and each of my children as we end the day together.

There was a time when I was giving the evening blessing to my daughter that didn't go as expected. I was sitting next to her on the bed and as I was giving her the blessing, she started to shake her head back and forth, and wrinkle up her nose. I said, "Lissy, I thought that you loved hearing me bless you?" She responded, "I like hearing it, not smelling it!" Apparently, my breath was not in top form that evening. So, if you are going to start blessing your kids before bed, brush your teeth!

Another powerful way to bless your children is to write down your prayers for them. Write down the blessings that you want to ask from God for the life of your son or daughter. A few months ago, I found an old "blessing letter" on my son's dresser. It was quite wrinkled. I asked him, out of curiosity, "RW, do you ever read that letter I gave you?" I was blown away by his answer. "Every day, Dad." Take the time to give your kids prayers and encouragement in writing. It makes a difference.

Which of these four God-given, power-packed moments would be the place for you to start increasing your spiritual life with your children?

> a) Sitting at home together.
> b) Transition times/travel time.
> c) At the start of the day.
> d) At the end of the day.

Don't get overwhelmed by all this. I believe that God wants us sharing spiritual life with our children multiple times every day. But it may have been months since you prayed with your kids apart from a meal time – and even longer since you read the Bible together.

Don't be discouraged! The past is the past. You can't go back, but you can go forward. God has a new future for you. Take a moment and pray right now and ask God where He would have you start. Which of these four power-moments of the day would God have you give special attention to this coming month? Choose one. Start small. Build a new habit.

In our next chapter, we are going to give our full attention to the first "power-moment" mentioned in Deuteronomy 6. What does it look like to "sit at home" with our families and talk about spiritual things? For many centuries this priority of spiritual time in the home has been called "family worship." In the last 100 years family worship has been all but lost. It is time to rediscover its beauty and its power to change our families by the grace of God.

REDISCOVERING FAMILY WORSHIP

When you were growing up, did your family regularly sit down together to read the Bible, sing and pray together? If you answered no, you are not alone. This spiritual time at home has historically been called "family worship." In surveying parents, I have found that about 25 percent grew up in a home where they had some type of family worship. Even then, only half of those who experienced family worship remember it as a positive experience. As a result, few of us have any positive models for establishing this in our own families.

Yet family worship can be fun. In fact, it can be one of the most eagerly anticipated times of the day for your kids! That's because family worship, as the engine that powers the spiritual life of the home, bonds the family together.

Imagine what wonderful things would happen if your family regularly explored the amazing truths of the Bible together. Think of how deeply your hearts would be connected through talking with the Creator of the universe in family prayer. What would life be like in a family that encouraged one another to grow in faith and character? All these things happen through family worship.

God desires us to prioritize this time into our schedule so that we might pass our faith to our children. In Psalm 78:5-7 we learn more about God's call for faith to be passed from one generation to the next.

> *He decreed statutes for Jacob and established the law in Israel, which He commanded our forefathers to teach their children, so the next generation would know them, even the children yet to be born, and they in turn would tell their children. Then they would put their trust in God and would not forget His deeds but would keep His commands.*

We have a tendency to think that the way Christianity is practiced today is the way it has always been. This is not true. For example, many Christian families today believe that the church (Sunday school, youth group, etc.) is primarily responsible for helping their children grow in faith. However, as we will see, the history of Christianity has primarily been one of home-centered, parent-centered approach to leading children in their faith.

Family Worship in the Early Church

Family worship was the teaching and practice of the early Christians. They believed that worship began in their homes. In fact, for the first decades of the early Church, there were no Christian church buildings at all.

If a person felt called to be a pastor in a church, he had to demonstrate that he was actively leading and teaching his children to love the Lord. It was a resume essential. [2]

The early Church believed that each household was like a small church, and that the head of the household was to be its spiritual shepherd. The home was to be a place of worship, spiritual life and service.[3]

Family Worship and the Reformation

During the Dark Ages and Middle Ages, literacy declined and people were not encouraged to read the Bible for themselves. However, with the invention of the printing press in the 1400s and the translation of the Bible into common languages, family worship was revived.

In 1556 John Knox wrote, "You must [share with] your family in reading Scripture, exhorting and in prayers,

[2] 1 Timothy 3:4 and Titus 1:6.
[3] John Chrysostom (AD 347-407), "Homily 36 on First Corinthians."

which I believe should be done in every house once a day, at least."[4]

Family Worship in Colonial Times

The Puritans, who were the spiritual founders of America, were totally committed to the practice of family worship. One of the primary responsibilities of church leaders in the 1600s was to visit each family in the community and to assess whether or not the parents were spiritually training their children through the regular practice of family worship. If they found that a family was not doing this, they would encourage the head of the household to begin. If, after that encouragement, the family still did not have family worship together, the parents of that household were not permitted to take communion! That consequence was to remain in effect until the parents demonstrated that they would now take seriously the spiritual training of their children.[5]

Why was family worship considered to be such a big deal? Because the Puritans understood that God's primary plan for reaching the next generation for Christ was the family … and that family worship was the spiritual engine of the home.

[4] John Knox, "Letter of Wholesome Counsel."
[5] "The Directory of Family Worship," Scotland 1640.

Family Worship in Modern Times

In the late 1800s, society moved from an agricultural way of life to an industrial one. Men now left the home to work away at the factory, rather than working near the home as a part of the family business. Kids also began leaving home more than ever before as public schools became widespread. In the 1900s, women increasingly began working outside the home as well. All these factors have combined to create a frequent cry from families today, "No one is ever home!"

Family worship is an uncommon thing in Christian homes today. Yet the Scriptures and Christian history call us to rediscover it. As God has changed my life during these past few years, I have become convinced that leading my family in worship is one of my most important responsibilities.

In the remainder of this chapter we will explore some of the key principles of family worship, along with some practical ways that your family can begin this powerful time in your home.

Principles of Family Worship

Principle #1: Family worship is the intersection of a right relationship with God and a right relationship with family.

I want everyone in my family to be growing in their love relationship with God. And by God's grace, that has begun to happen. In the same way, I want all our relationships within the family to be healthy, close and loving. We have plenty of arguments and problems, but God continues to help us. When we are gathered together for family worship, we are seeking to be right "vertically" (with God) and "horizontally" (with one another).

Principle #2: Family worship is the foundation for worship in church.

If children do not regularly experience worship in the home, how can we expect them to feel comfortable in church on Sunday mornings? Without family worship, that hour on Sundays is the most bizarre hour of the week. All of a sudden they are expected to sit, listen, sing, follow along in their Bibles and turn the attention of their hearts to spiritual things.

The reason that many children "can't sit still" in church services has nothing to do with the so-called "short attention span." It is most often a simple matter of a lack of training. When kids are a part of regular family worship in the home, parents are able to say to them on Sunday mornings, "This morning we are going to worship with our BIG family!" I am not saying that practicing family worship is a guarantee that your child will love church, but rather that worship on Sundays will not feel weird to them. Family worship helps you lay the foundation for a lifetime of worship in the local church.

Principle #3: Family worship will be a key target of the enemy.

If sitting together in your home and talking about spiritual things is one of God's central callings for your family, then Satan will do everything he can to prevent it from happening. You will be attacked by feelings of inadequacy. "You can't teach the Bible. You can't lead spiritual discussions. You don't even have your own act together." He will throw crazy schedules at you. Be prepared for kids crying and whining at exactly the wrong times.

However, I can promise you – based on the Bible – that God will equip and empower you to do this. God never calls us to do something and then abandons us when we seek to be obedient.

Making Changes

Family worship has been at the heart of Christian homes for centuries. How would your family change and grow if you spent more time together turning your hearts to the things of God? God calls us to family worship because it draws us closer to Him, keeps us close with one another and prepares our children to make a difference in the world for Christ.

In the next chapter, you will learn a variety of ways to create memorable and meaningful times of worship in your home.

PRACTICING FAMILY WORSHIP

Set a Reasonable Goal

Some people will come away from reading this book and, by the grace of God, will be inspired to begin family worship. They will make the big announcement to the family, "Starting tomorrow, we will all meet in the living room at 6:00 a.m. for an hour of family worship, and we are never going to miss a day for as long as we live!"

I love the passion, but you know what is going to happen. Tomorrow, the family will get out of bed at 5:59 a.m. and do their best to hang in there during the family worship time. The next day a few people will be late; it won't go as well as it did the first day and with that the commitment to family worship is over.

The commitment to family worship must be a long-term one. God wants us to slowly and steadily build this family foundation into our lives. That means we may have to start small. Set a reasonable goal that you know you can accomplish. Simply set your goal for more than you are doing now. If this will be a new adventure for you, the goal could be one family worship time each week. If you are currently having a family worship time once a week, set your goal for twice a week or more.

My desire is to have a time of family worship every day. (This would not include prayers before meals and going to bed.) I am not there yet, but I have a goal!

The schedules that we establish for our families teach the hearts of our children what is really important. Our calendars announce our priorities. So, if we don't have time for family worship because we are always running from one sports practice, music lesson or art class to the other, what does that teach our kids about what we value? Even great activities such as church programs can crowd out the priority of family worship if they have family members going in too many different directions.

Once you decide on how often you will have family worship, try to write the dates and times on the calendar. I know what happens when I say I am going to do something, "when I have time." That is code for, "I am probably never going to do this." Write it down. Post it on the fridge. Protect that time just like you would an important meeting or kid's ball game.

Mix It Up

Here are some key components that you can mix and match together to keep your family worship times fresh.

Reading and Responding to the Bible

This can be a simple time where one member of the family reads a few paragraphs from the Bible. Perhaps you have never read the Bible on your own. Family Bible reading will be a great place to start your own journey! I encourage you to begin with the book of Mark in the New Testament. It is an "action-packed" account of the life of Jesus and will create great discussions for your family.

In my family, we tend to read through one book from the Bible at a time, rather than jump around each time we read. After the Scripture passage has been read, we see if anyone has any questions. Little children may not know what a particular word means. Others may have questions of curiosity. Answering these questions is a natural, confidence-building teaching opportunity for you as a parent.

Your kids may ask questions that you *don't* know how to answer. Don't panic. There is a great response for this: "I don't know." The purpose of reading the Bible together as a family is not to demonstrate that you know everything, but rather to point ourselves toward the one who actually does.

Invite each person to respond, from their heart, to what they heard. It is important for the adults to set the example with this. For instance, we were recently reading a part of the story of Jacob and Esau in the book of Genesis. The character trait of jealousy was a major cause of the problems in that family. After we did our reading for the day, I shared about some jealous feelings that I was having toward someone in my life, and I asked the family to pray for me that God would give me contentment.

Make sure that family Bible reading is not viewed by the kids as "Bible class." Yes, there will be times that you are teaching your kids what certain verses mean and how they apply to life. But the goal of family Bible reading is not merely instruction; it is life transformation. We need to set the example for our kids by putting ourselves under the authority of the Bible, allowing it to speak to our hearts, and letting our kids hear us talk about it.

Begin even if your children are young. Place your infant on your lap and simply begin reading. Give your toddler a few toys to play with on the floor and read the Bible aloud. I think of it like a "Bible spa" for little ones. God's words fill the air, and I believe His power is at work even when we can't see it.

Remember, even if young children are not understanding some or all of what they hear, you are still developing a critical family discipline that will be "the norm" in their lives as they grow older.

Praying for One Another

If you want to create a home that is saturated with the presence of God, then pray frequently together. Do you pray together before your meals? If not, this is a great place to start adding prayer to your family life. Encourage different people to pray at each meal, and try not to rush through your prayer just to get to the food. This is another important time of modeling the right attitude toward God in prayer. When it is your turn to pray before eating, take it seriously. Your kids will learn a lot about how to relate to God from the tone of voice you use when you pray.

Praying together as a family before bed is a meaningful way to end your day. Yes, the minutes before bed can be very hectic. You may be eager to get all the kids to bed so you can take care of some things around the house.

Remember, however, that one of the four power-moments for discipleship is right before bed. Sit with your kids on their bed, encourage them to pray and then pray yourself. I know many teenagers who look forward to this time with their parents, because it has been a part of their relationship from the beginning. If you have teenagers and you have never done this sort of thing, don't be afraid to try it. It will be awkward at first, but what could be more important?

Another way to build prayer into the life of your family is to share prayer requests with each other. At the breakfast table, go around the circle and ask each person to share a request. Have each person pray for the person on their right, offering their request to God. At the end of the day, be sure to get reports on how God answered. Consider getting a small whiteboard where family prayer requests can be written down. This will keep your family prayer life visible throughout the day.

Singing Together

Singing worship songs together as a family is a time-honored Christian tradition. Don't be afraid to try – the goal is not to sound like a choir! You don't need to have a rehearsal before you start. The way this works in our home is that someone chooses a song that he or she likes, and we just start singing! I can assure you that a recording of our family singing would never sell a single copy, due entirely to my vocal contribution.

I realize that the idea of singing together may seem outdated. If your kids are older, and you have never done this, it may be a difficult place to start. However, there are many ways to incorporate singing and music into your times of family worship.

If your children are younger, visit a Christian bookstore and get a worship DVD, kids' praise songbook or hymnal or a praise CD. Give different family members the opportunity to choose the songs that you will sing. Little ones may enjoy using their toy instruments. If you have elementary or older kids who have learned how to play instruments, invite them to use their gifts to help the family worship God through music.

One idea for middle- or high-school students is to invite them to bring one of their favorite Christian songs to the family worship time. Invite them to play the song for the family, listen together with a worshipful heart and discuss the lyrics together.

Experiences and Object Lessons

Family worship is not supposed to be dull and boring! Creating fun, memorable experiences helps everyone in the family look forward to family worship and benefit from it. Putting time and energy into creative games and object lessons is worth the effort. Thankfully, there are people who have already put their time and energy into coming up with these fun family worship activities. Here are a few ideas from Family Time Training[6] that we have used with our kids.

Running the Race for God

Before your family worship time, set up a racecourse around the house. If the weather is lousy, you can do this inside. Have one room be the "starting line" and have the kids run from there to another room on the other side of the house and back again. Find a watch with a second hand, and give each of the kids a chance to run the course a few times so that they can get their best possible time.

After everyone has had a couple of turns running the course, bring out a box of winter clothes. Have the kids put on as many layers of winter clothes as they can. Oversized snowsuits and big boots are particularly effective! Once they are loaded up with the winter clothing, have

---

[6] Family Time Training exists to train families to teach children Christian principles and values in the home. Visit www.famtime.com to learn more.

them run the racecourse again. They will have a great time stumbling their way through it. (If you are doing it indoors, be sure that Grandma's vintage china is far away from the course.) Because of all the clothes that they are wearing, it will take them longer to finish the race. After they have had the chance to get their best times, change back into normal clothes and gather the family together.

Open your Bible and read Hebrews 12:1-2a.

Therefore, since we are surrounded by such a great cloud of witnesses, let us throw off everything that hinders and the sin that so easily entangles, and let us run with perseverance the race marked out for us. Let us fix our eyes on Jesus, the author and perfecter of our faith.

After reading, you can explain the experience in this way. "Kids, I hope you had a good time with the racecourse. The reason we did that was so we could remember the lesson from Hebrews 12. God has a plan for each one of our lives. That is like the racecourse that we set up for you. He wants you to follow His path for your life. He wants you to run hard for Him. But just like the winter clothes slowed you down in our race, there is something that will slow you down in running for God. In the verse that

I just read, what does it say slows us down in running for God? Sin. When we choose to disobey God, we fall off the course. God brought us together as a family so we could help each other sin less and run fast for God. If we want to run for God, and get rid of sin, we have to fix our eyes on Jesus. Let's do that right now by praying together and confessing our sins to God and asking Him to help us to run for Him."

The Quicksand

We shared this activity with a group of families at our house. We gathered all the kids on a tile area at the bottom of our stairs. There were 17 kids, ranging from ages 2 to 10, packed into a small area. We then said to them, "Do any of you know what quicksand is?" Some of the older ones raised their hands and informed the group. "Yes, that's right. Quicksand is very dangerous stuff, and the tile that you are sitting on IS quicksand! Your mission is to get to safety, and the only safe place is at the top of the stairs where some of the dads are. You have to find a way to get up there. There are a couple of rules. First, you can't touch the stairs. Second, you can't touch the railings on the stairs. You have five minutes to figure this out. Go!"

At this point, the kids' eyes were all wide with panic. For two minutes they were batting around ideas for how to save themselves from the dreaded quicksand. Then, one boy stood up and called up to his dad, "Dad, come get me!" His father walked down the stairs, picked him up, brought him to the top of the stairs and set him down … safe and sound. The other kids all looked at each other and realized it had worked. All the kids then stood up and called for their dads to come down and get them. I was tired after going down and up four times to rescue each of my children.

After everyone had been saved, all the families sat down together and we opened the Bible to Psalm 40:1-2.

> *I waited patiently for the LORD; He turned to me and heard my cry. He lifted me out of the slimy pit, out of the mud and mire; He set my feet on a rock and gave me a firm place to stand.*

One of the parents then said, "Kids, the reason that we did that quicksand game was so that you would remember something very important. There was only one way to get to the top of the stairs, and out of the quicksand, and that joy and peace. Which of these nine things do you want most for God to develop in your life?" After discussing this question, encourage each person to pray, asking for God to bring that character trait into his or her heart.

Family Worship With Teenagers

A friend of mine recently tried to lead his first-ever time of family worship. His girls are in their teens. Needless to say, he was not sure how they would respond. After 45 minutes of great discussion and some prayer, his teenage daughter said, "Dad, why did we wait so long to do this?" It is never too late!

If you begin family worship when your kids are young, moving into the teenage years will not be so difficult. However, if you are starting with older kids, here are some principles that will help you be successful.

Principle #1: Honesty is the best policy.

Tell your teenagers that you have failed to provide something that is very important to the family. Apologize that you have not set aside time for the family to talk about spiritual things. Show the family what it says in Deuteronomy 6 and in Ephesians 6. Tell them that you would like to start doing your best to follow what God says by having some times of family worship.

Principle #2: Make it a team effort.

Invite your teenagers into the planning and leadership of the worship time. Tell them you want their help so that this time isn't boring or irrelevant. Invite them to choose the Scriptures that you read. Ask them to figure out how best to design the prayer time. Give them the freedom to choose some of the worship songs.

Part of the motivation for this involvement is to help your teenager feel a sense of ownership for what is happening now. But just as important, you are training them for leading family worship in their own homes someday. And be sure to emphasize with your teenagers the opportunity to include their friends in family worship when they are in your home. Yes, it's countercultural – but don't underestimate the spiritual power of a caring family atmosphere compared with the emptiness of youth culture. God could use your family worship time in a meaningful way.

Principle #3: Don't be discouraged.

Starting family worship with teenagers will be challenging. They may not feel comfortable opening up their spiritual

Start *somewhere*. Set your heart to the mission God has given you – to impress the hearts of your children with a love for Him. He will give you all the strength, time and creativity you need!

In my journey to lead my children and family closer to Christ, I have become painfully aware that I need lots of help. I need constant encouragement from others. I need motivation, creative ideas and prayer. If you want to embrace this mission to make your home into a discipleship center, don't do it alone. In the next chapter, we will talk about some great ways to build a support team around your family.

DON'T GO ALONE | 7

DON'T GO ALONE

This mission of family discipleship is far too important to attempt alone. The pressures and distractions of the world will continually pull your heart and your attention away from the spiritual training of your children. Transforming your home into a discipleship center is not going to happen overnight. We need all the help we can get. Here are three ways you can find encouragement, partner with other parents and stay focused on the journey ahead.

Awana® at Home™

Awana helps churches and parents raise children and youth to know, love and serve Jesus Christ. (Your child may already be involved in Awana Clubs. If not, visit www.awana.org to learn more and find a church in your area that has an Awana ministry.)

Awana developed the Awana at Home ministry to proclaim and promote the following values:

- Parents are called by God to be the primary spiritual nurturers of their kids.

- The church plays a critical supporting role, encouraging and equipping parents to be what God called them to be.

- Maximum disciple-making power is achieved when parents and the church work in tandem, each fulfilling the role God created for it.

By integrating with a church's Awana Clubs program, Awana at Home creates an environment of community and accountability for parents along with opportunities for celebration and support. The program also gives parents the training and tools to establish and execute a plan for spiritually developing their children.

Be sure to talk with your church leadership about Awana at Home. More information is available at www.awana.org/athome. And if your church does not currently use the Awana Clubs ministry, I encourage you to consider it. Not only is it a proven way to reach kids in your community, but it will be a great help to parents as well.

Partner With Other Families

Are there one or two other families that would join with you in your mission to have Christ at the center of your family life? Consider bringing a few families together once a month for a time of building friendships and spiritual growth together. Here is a schedule for how a family gathering might work:

30 minutes – families arrive – kids play

45 minutes – easy prep/easy cleanup dinner

30 minutes – family worship

45 minutes – adult discussion time - kids play

Visionary Parenting

My wife Amy and I would love to encourage and support you in your parenting journey. We have developed an eight-part workshop for parents and grandparents called Visionary Parenting. These eight sessions inspire you from the Bible about God's plan for your family. You will also learn practical, everyday tools for dealing with difficult discipline situations, building confidence in the hearts of your kids, creating a balanced family schedule and more.

You can listen to messages from the Visionary Parenting series and find many other resources at www.visionaryparenting.com. The entire workshop is available on DVD for use in small groups or for an adult class at your church.

CONCLUSION

I pray that as you have read this book, the Lord has inspired you to impress the hearts of your kids with a love for God. God gave you your children so that you would help them get safely home to their Father in heaven and prepare them to make a difference for Christ in this lost world. Your greatest impact on this world will be the children that you release into it.

The world is filled with pain and problems. Skim the front page of the paper and you will find war, poverty and injustice. How can people like us impact such huge problems? What can make a difference?

The world doesn't need more smart people. It doesn't need more athletic people. It doesn't need more musical people. It doesn't even need more famous people. These things are fine, but they are not the answer. The world needs more people who love Jesus more than anything, and who will bring His love and compassion to everyone they meet. When we raise up the next generation to live for Him, we do our part to fill the earth with witnesses of God's glory and grace.

Remember that God is not calling you to a new checklist of things to do. Checklists come and go. Rather, He is calling you to be the primary spiritual leader and guide for your kids. Will you accept this role? Will you give the best of your time, energy and creativity to the spiritual life of your family?

I pray that when we come to the end of our lives, we will all be able to echo the words written by the apostle John.

I have no greater joy than to hear that my children are walking in the truth. (3 John 4)

ABOUT THE AUTHOR

Dr. Rob Rienow has been married to his wife Amy since 1994. They have been blessed with six children. His family is his most important ministry. He has served as a pastor at Wheaton Bible Church in West Chicago, Illinois since 1992, currently in the role of Family Pastor.

Rob has an M.A. in Theology from Wheaton College Graduate School, an M.Div. from Trinity International University, and a Doctor of Ministry degree in Christian Leadership from Gordon-Conwell Theological Seminary. Amy has an M.A. in clinical psychology, and is a licensed professional counselor.

Rob, Amy and family live in Wheaton, Illinois.

Together, Rob and Amy founded Visionary Parenting, a ministry designed to:

- Inspire parents to impress the hearts of their kids with a love for God.

- Equip churches to develop home-centered, biblical strategies for reaching the coming generations for Christ.

Visit www.visionaryparenting.com for more information and resources to help you.